CAMBRIDGE
UNIVERSITY PRESS

CAMBRIDGE
Primary Science

Workbook 3

Jon Board & Alan Cross

CAMBRIDGE
UNIVERSITY PRESS

University Printing House, Cambridge CB2 8BS, United Kingdom

One Liberty Plaza, 20th Floor, New York, NY 10006, USA

477 Williamstown Road, Port Melbourne, VIC 3207, Australia

314–321, 3rd Floor, Plot 3, Splendor Forum, Jasola District Centre,
New Delhi – 110025, India

103 Penang Road, #05–06/07, Visioncrest Commercial, Singapore 238467

Cambridge University Press is part of the University of Cambridge.

It furthers the University's mission by disseminating knowledge in the pursuit of
education, learning and research at the highest international levels of excellence.

www.cambridge.org
Information on this title: www.cambridge.org/9781108742771

First published 2014

Second edition 2021

20 19 18 17 16 15 14 13 12 11 10 9 8

Printed in India by Multivista Global Pvt Ltd

A catalogue record for this publication is available from the British Library

ISBN 9781108742771 Paperback with Digital Access (1 Year)

The exercises in this Workbook have been written to cover the Biology, Chemistry,
Physics, Earth and Space and any appropriate Thinking and Working Scientifically
learning objectives from the Cambridge Primary Science curriculum framework
(0097). Some Thinking and Working Scientifically learning objectives and the
Science in Context learning objectives have not been covered in this Workbook.

Contents

How to use this book

1 Plants are living things

1.1	Alive or not alive?	2
1.2	Plant parts	7
1.3	Plants and light	10
1.4	Plants need water and the right temperature	13

2 Mixing materials

2.1	Solids, liquids and gases	17
2.2	Separating mixtures	20
2.3	Dissolving	23
2.4	Filtering	27
2.5	Separating materials from rocks	30

3 Light and shadows

3.1	Shadows	34
3.2	Changing shadows	37
3.3	Transparent materials	40
3.4	Translucent materials	43

4 Staying alive

4.1	Human organs	46
4.2	Animal groups and different life cycles	49
4.3	Food chains	53
4.4	Fossils	58

5 Forces and magnets

5.1	Forces and forcemeters	62
5.2	Gravity	65
5.3	Friction	68
5.4	Amazing magnets	72
5.5	Magnetic materials	75

6 The Earth and the Moon

6.1	The shape of the Earth, Sun and Moon	78
6.2	The Moon	81
6.3	The phases of the Moon	83

How to use this book

This workbook provides questions for you to practise what you have learned in class. There is a topic to match each topic in your Learner's Book. Each topic contains the following sections:

Focus: these questions help you to master the basics ⟶

Practice: these questions help you to become more confident in using what you have learned

Challenge: these questions will make you think more deeply ⟶

Focus

1 Colour in **only** the things that are alive.

Practice

2 Write the words in the right box.

| small leaves | big leaves | tall stem |

Plants with light	Plants in the dark
_____	_____
_____	_____
_____	_____

Challenge

Use the words to finish the sentences.

| alive | not alive |

Example: A ball is not alive.

A fish is _____.

A rock is _____.

A cat can _____.

A cat is _____.

The Sun does not need _____.

The Sun is _____.

| alive | not alive |
| food | move |

1 Use the words to finish the sentences.

1 ▶ Plants are living things

⟩ 1.1 Alive or not alive?

Focus

1 Look at these pictures. Draw each one in the correct group in the table.

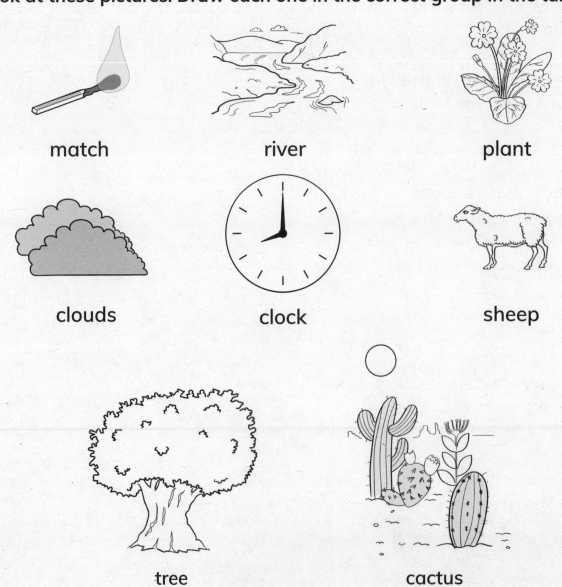

match

river

plant

clouds

clock

sheep

tree

cactus

Alive	Not alive

Practice

These are the seven rules to tell if something is a living thing.

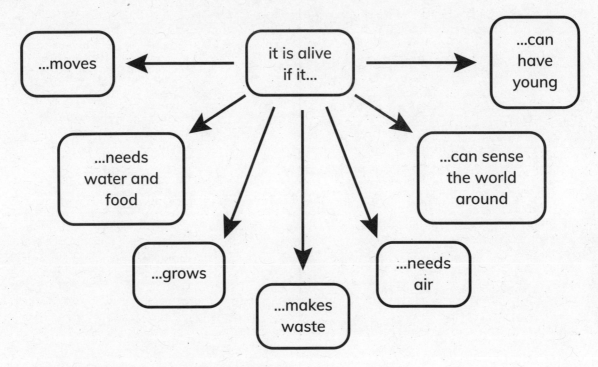

2 a Look at the things in the table.
Use the rules to decide if they are alive or not.

	Moves	Needs water and food	Grows	Makes waste	Needs air	Can sense	Has young	Alive
A goat	✓	✓	✓	✓	✓	✓	✓	✓
A cat								
The Moon								
A tree								
A dolphin								
An ant								

b Complete these sentences using your answers from the table.
   Pick one thing that is alive and one thing that is not alive.

   A I know _____ is alive because _____ .

   B I know _____ is not alive because _____ .

Challenge

Look at the pictures below.

plastic building block

rain

wood

fan

frog spawn

crab

rock

tree

3 a Sort the things shown in the picture into the three groups shown in the table below.

b Draw each thing in the correct box.

Living things	Things that were once alive	Things that have never been alive

4 Draw an object of your own in each box.

> 1.2 Plant parts

Focus

1 Colour this plant and label it.

Use these words.
roots   flower   leaf   stem

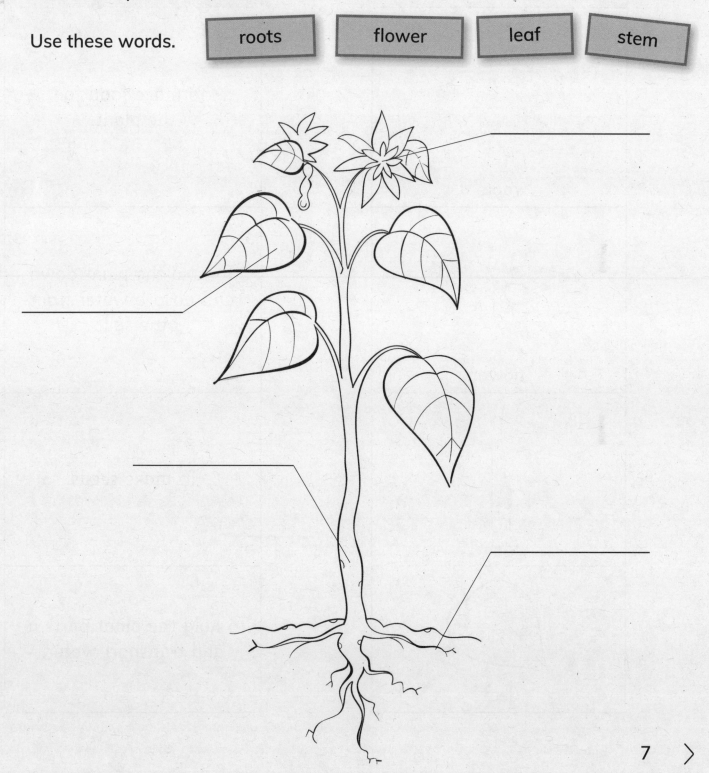

Practice

Every part of the plant is important.

2 Draw an arrow from the plant part to its important job.

Plant part	Important job
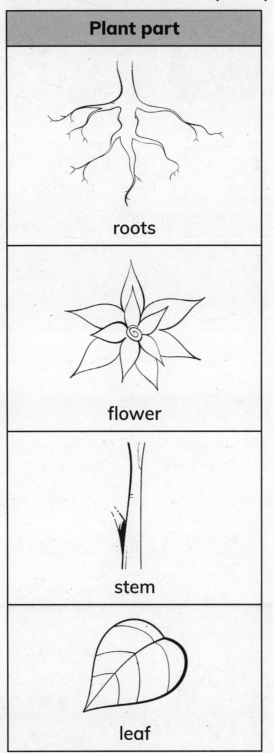	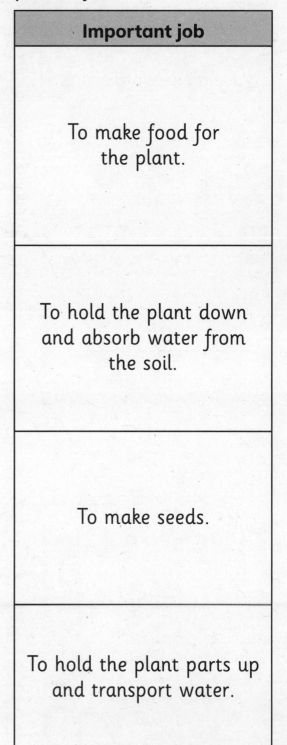

Challenge

Sofia wonders what would happen if a plant did not have all these plant parts: roots, flower, stem, leaf.

3   Write in the bubbles what you think would happen to a plant without these plant parts.

roots

flower

stem

leaf

> 1.3 Plants and light

Focus

Four similar plants are put in different places.

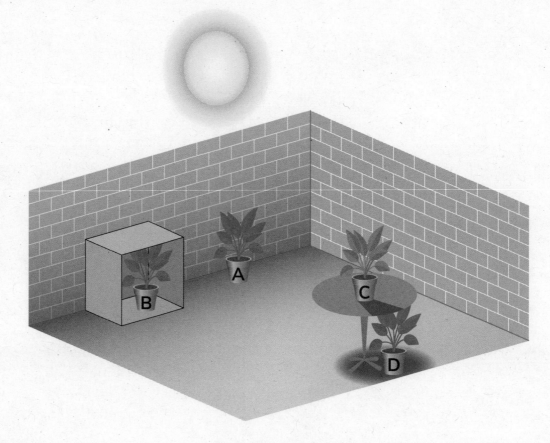

1   Look at the picture and answer the questions. Use the letters A, B, C or D.

   a   Plant _____ will grow well because it has most light.

   b   Plants _____ , _____ and _____ will
       grow less well because they have less light.

   c   Plant _____ would grow better if it was moved

       next to plant _____ .

Practice

Two similar plants are growing.
One is in the light, the other is in a dark box.

The plants have water.

2   Draw what happens to the plants as they begin to grow.

Plant with light

Plant with no light

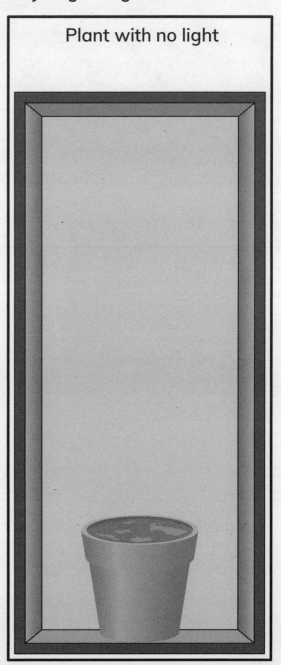

Challenge

Look at the four seeds below and the places they will grow.
They all get enough water, but will they grow well?

3 Look at the pictures and complete the sentences in the questions.

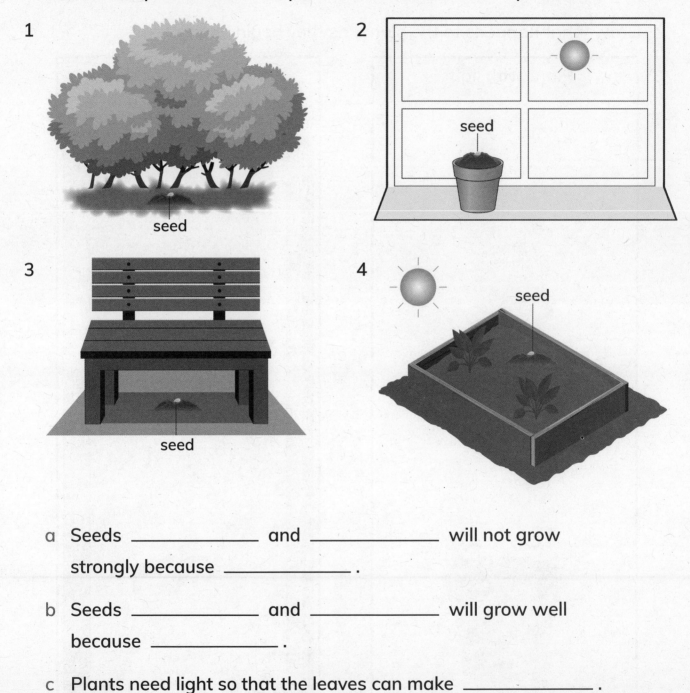

1

2

3

4

a Seeds _____ and _____ will not grow
strongly because _____ .

b Seeds _____ and _____ will grow well
because _____ .

c Plants need light so that the leaves can make _____ .

> 1.4 Plants need water and the right temperature

Focus

Plants need the right amount of water.

They also need the right temperature.

Look at these pictures. Is each plant growing well?

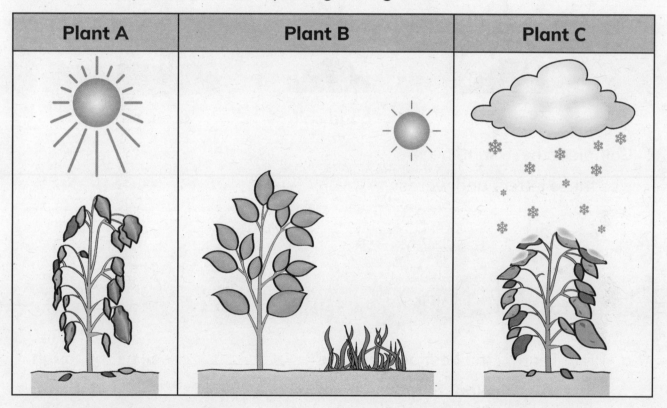

Plant A	Plant B	Plant C

1   Read these sentences.

   Complete them by adding the right letter A, B or C.

   a   Plant _____ cannot grow well because it is too cold.

   b   Plant _____ cannot grow well because it is too hot.

   c   Plant _____ can grow well because it has the right temperature.

Practice

Three seeds were grown in different places.

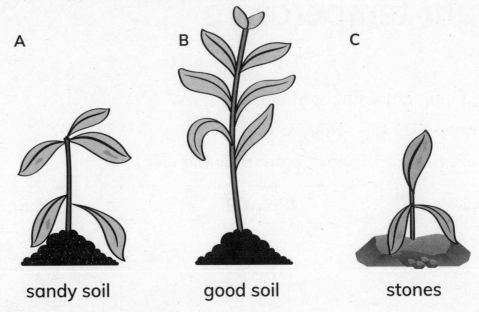

A   B   C

sandy soil   good soil   stones

2   Complete these sentences.

Use these letters and words.

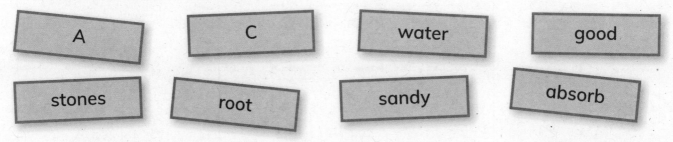

A   C   water   good

stones   root   sandy   absorb

a   Plant B grew the best because the _____ soil held enough

water for the plant to grow. The root could _____ enough

water from the soil.

b   Plant C grew the least because the _____

had no water. The root could not absorb any _____ .

c   Plant A grew a little because the root absorbed a little water.

The _____ soil holds only a little water.

Challenge

Arun had two plants that were the same.
He gave water to one plant.
He did not give water to the other plant.

Every day he measured the height of the plants.

Here are the results on day 1 and day 10.

Height	With water (cm)	No water (cm)
Day 1	4	4
Day 10	8	3

3 a   Draw the bar charts for each day.

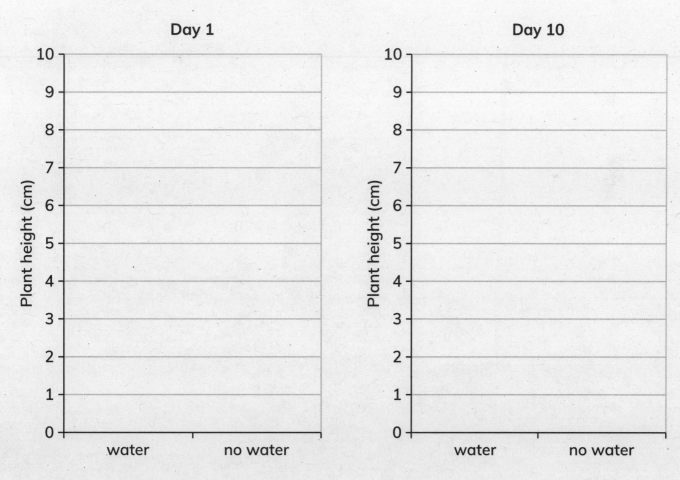

b Which plant grew better? _____

Why?

_____

_____

c How tall do you think the plant with water was on day 5?

_____

_____

2 ▶ Mixing materials

❯ 2.1 Solids, liquids and gases

Focus

1   Label the things in the picture as solid, a liquid or gas.

6 _____

4 _____

5 _____

1 _____

2 _____

3 _____

8 _____

7 _____

Practice

2 Sort these materials into solid, liquid and gas groups.

Add another material to each group.

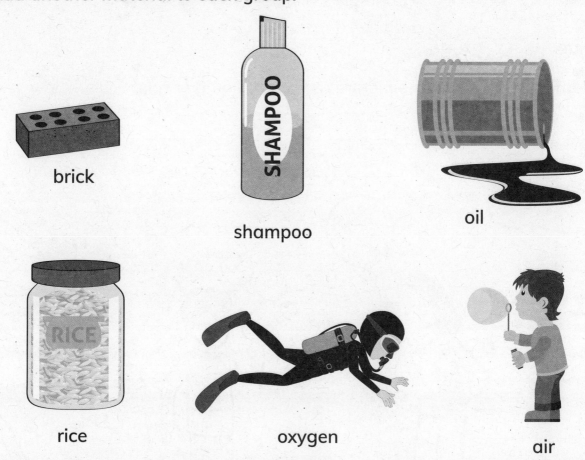

brick

shampoo

oil

rice

oxygen

air

Solid	Liquid	Gas

Challenge

3 Use these words to finish the sentences.

| liquid | solid |

a A _____ stays the same shape unless it is compressed, stretched, twisted or bent.

b A _____ changes shape easily.

Use these words to finish the sentences.

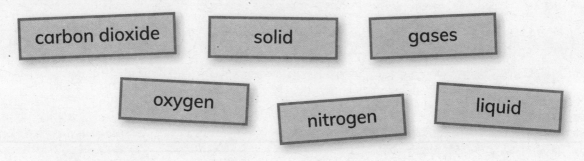

| carbon dioxide | solid | gases |

| oxygen | nitrogen | liquid |

c Humans breathe a gas called _____ .

d Vinegar is a _____ .

e Bicarbonate of soda is a _____ .

f Mixing vinegar and bicarbonate of soda makes a gas called

_____ .

g Air is a mixture of _____ .

h Most of the air is a gas called _____ .

⟩ 2.2 Separating mixtures

Focus

1 Label these diagrams.

Use these words.

mixture   magnet   mixture   sieve

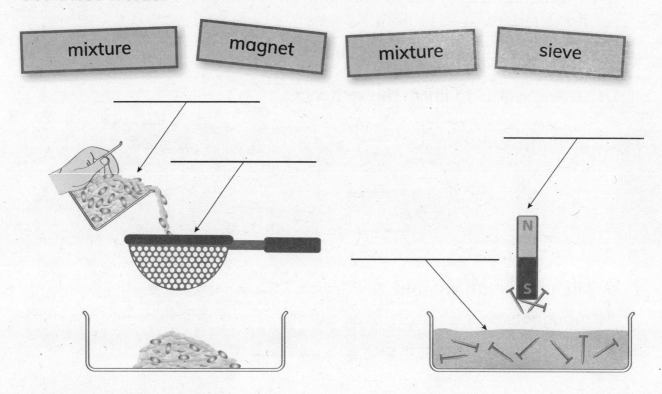

2 Fill in the missing words.

Use these words.

magnet   separate   separate   sieve

a We can use a _____ to _____ a mixture
of rice and beans.

b We can use a _____ to _____ a mixture
of metal pins and sand.

Practice

3 a Draw lines to match each mixture to the sieve that can be used to separate it.

   b Finish each sentence.

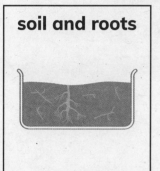

soil and roots

The _____ will go through the holes but the _____ will not.

rice and sand

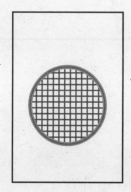

The _____ will go through the holes but the _____ will not.

rice and beans

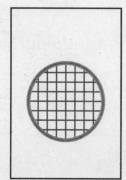

The _____ will go through the holes but the _____ will not.

Challenge

Zara has drawn two diagrams to show how she separated a mixture of sand and rocks.

Diagram 1

Sand

← Cup

Our mixture

Diagram 2

Rocks do not go through the holes

← Plate

Look at Zara's diagrams.
She has made some mistakes.

She has not labelled all the equipment and all the materials in each diagram. Some of her diagram is not neat.

4 a What mistake has she made in diagram 1?

_____

b What three mistakes has she made in diagram 2?

1 _____

2 _____

3 _____

> 2.3 Dissolving

Focus

1 Add the missing words to these sentences.

Use these words.

dissolve   soluble   insoluble   transparent   insoluble

a Sand is _____ in water.

b Salt is _____ in cooking oil.

c Salt is _____ in water.

d The more water there is, the more salt can _____ .

e When a solid dissolves in water the solid cannot be seen but

the water is still _____ .

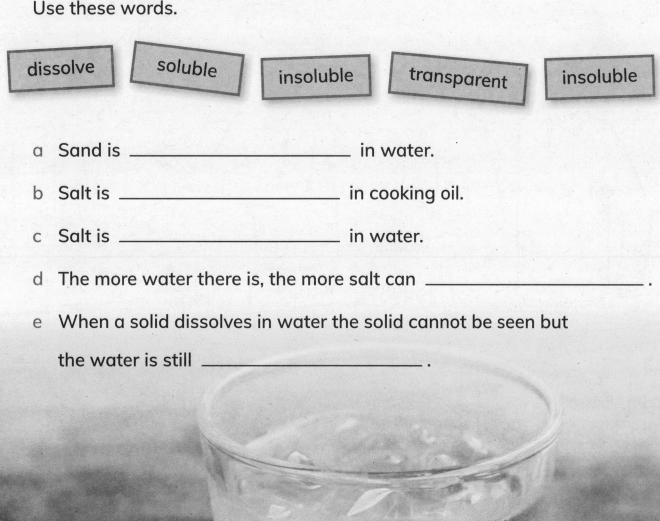

Practice

These children are doing an investigation that is unsafe.

2 (Circle) three things that are dangerous.

3 Write two things these children should not do.

_____

_____

_____

_____

Challenge

Zara and Marcus have investigated a science question.

Does more sugar dissolve when the water is warmer?

Here are their results.

Temperature of water	Number of teaspoons of sugar that dissolved
Cold	1
Warm	3
Hot	5

4 a How many teaspoons of sugar dissolved in the warm water?

_____

b How many more teaspoons of sugar dissolved in the hot water

than the cold water? _____

c Does more sugar dissolve when the water is warmer? _____

d Marcus and Zara were doing a fair test.
What was the one thing they changed?

_____

_____

e What was the one thing they measured?

_____

_____

f Write one thing they kept the same to make their test fair.

_____

_____

> 2.4 Filtering

Focus

1 Write the correct sentence for each picture.

| Pour the mixture into the filter paper. | Put the filter paper into the funnel. | Put a cup under the funnel. |

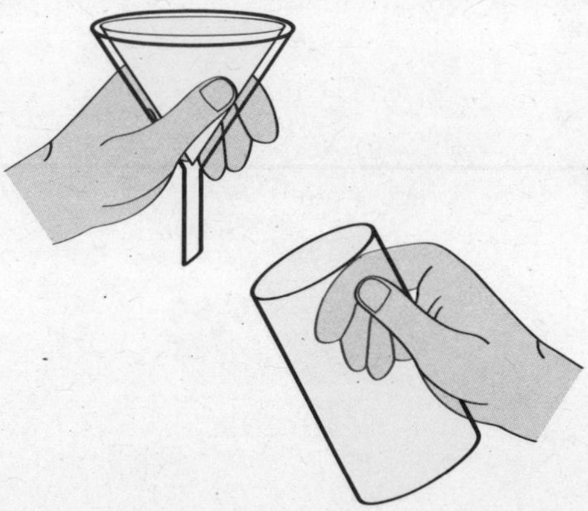

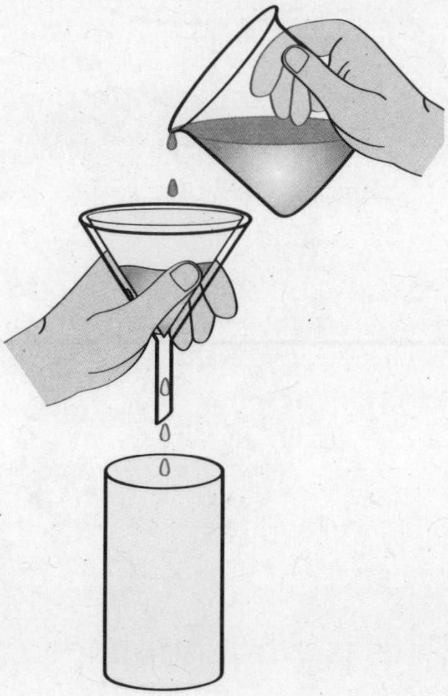

_____

_____

_____

_____

_____

_____

_____

_____

_____

_____

_____

_____

Practice

Sofia, Marcus and Zara are filtering dirty water.
They all make different predictions.

The water will be less dirty when it comes out.

The water will still be very dirty when it comes out.

The water will come out clean.

Zara   Marcus   Sofia

This is what happened.

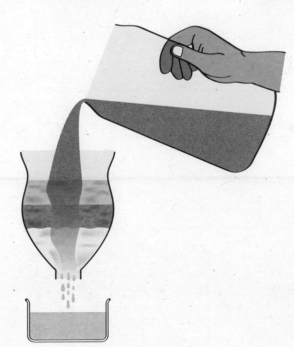

2 a Was Sofia's prediction correct? _____

  b How do you know? _____

3 a Was Marcus's prediction correct? _____

  b How do you know? _____

4 Was Zara's prediction correct? _____

Challenge

Can these mixtures be separated using a filter?

5 a Water and sugar _____

  b How do you know? _____

  _____

6 a Vinegar and salt _____

  b How do you know? _____

  _____

7 a Cooking oil and salt _____

  b How do you know? _____

  _____

> 2.5 Separating materials from rocks

Focus

1 Complete the grid using your answers to the questions below.

a A material made from oil. (7 letters)

b A gas that causes global warming. (6 letters/7 letters)

c Materials that are not made but are found on planet Earth. (7 letters)

d Metals are made from these. (4 letters)

e This material is a fuel. (6 letters)

f Making metal is called _____ (8 letters)

Practice

2 a Name three fuels.

_____

_____

_____

  b What material do fuels contain? _____

  c What happens when fuels are burned?

_____

_____

  d Give an example of humans burning fuel.

_____

_____

  e Why is global warming a problem?

_____

_____

_____

_____

_____

Challenge

Cobalt mining

Cobalt is a metal used to make batteries for mobile phones and electric cars. Cobalt ore is mined in a country called the Democratic Republic of Congo, in Africa. Many people who live there are very poor. Children work in the mines to make money to live. They are not paid very much for the work. The mines are not safe so the children can get hurt or can become ill. Some children who work in the mine are only seven years old. They break the rocks to separate the cobalt ore from the rock.

Some people who make mobile phones and electric cars try not to buy cobalt from mines that use children. Others do not find out where the cobalt they buy comes from.

3 a What kind of material is cobalt? _____

   b What is cobalt used for?

   _____

   _____

   c How do they separate the cobalt ore from the rocks?

   _____

   _____

   d Why do the children work in the mine?

   _____

   _____

   e What could people who buy mobile phones or electric cars do to help?

   _____

   _____

   _____

   _____

   _____

3 ▶ Light and shadows

> 3.1 Shadows

Focus

1 Look at the objects below.

   Draw a line to match each object to the right shadow.

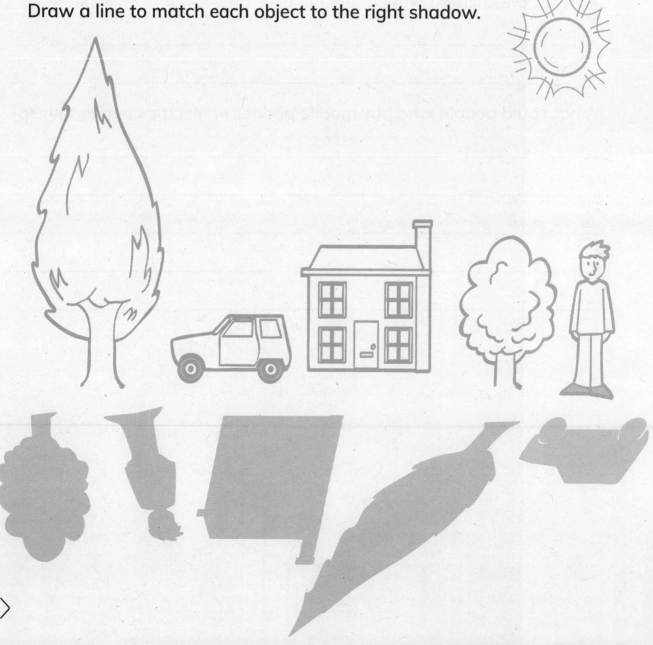

Practice

2 Look at these objects. Predict the shadow shape and draw it on the right.

Object	Drawing of the shadow
ruler	
paper clip	
book	
comb	
tracing paper	

Challenge

3   Look at the objects. Has each shadow been drawn correctly?

Write a tick (✓) or cross (✗) to say if the shadow is right or wrong.

If the shadow is wrong, draw it correctly at the bottom.

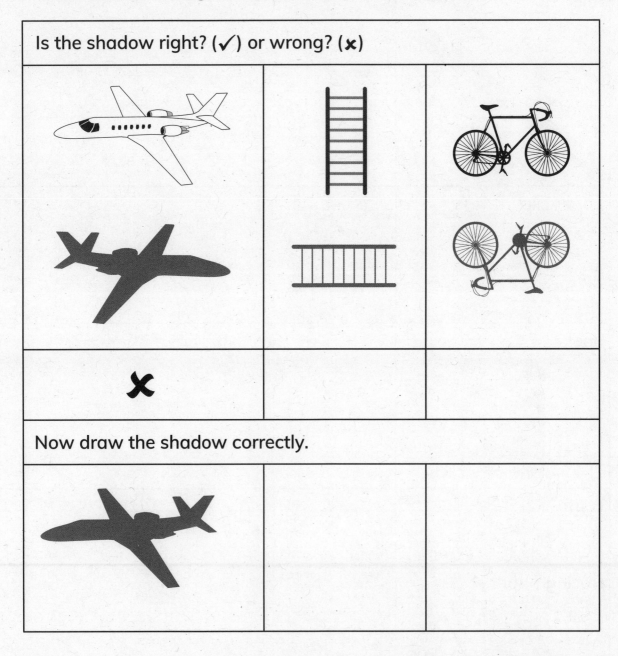

Is the shadow right? (✓) or wrong? (✗)

Now draw the shadow correctly.

> 3.2 Changing shadows

Focus

1 Here are four objects. Draw one shadow each object might make.
Then draw a different shadow the object might make.

Object	Shadow 1	Shadow 2
Paper clip		
Pencil		
Phone		
Scissors		
Cell		

Practice

At noon the Sun is high and Kamal has a very short shadow.

2 a Draw the Sun lower in the sky near the X at 4pm.

  b Draw what Kamal's shadow will look like at 4pm.

4 pm

Challenge

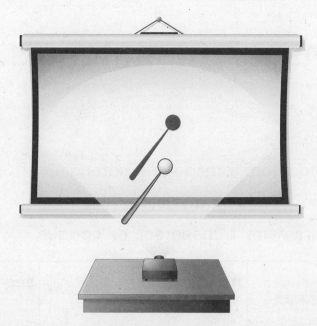

Marcus measured the size of a shadow as he moved a drumstick towards a light source.

He recorded his results on the table below.

3 Look at the table and answer the questions.

Test number	Distance from light source (cm)	Size of shadow (cm)
1	50	6
2	40	14
3	30	25
4	20	34
5	10	42

a For each test Marcus moved the drumstick _____ cm closer to the light source.

b The shadow was biggest when the drumstick was _____ cm from the light source.

c What is the pattern in the shadow size? Complete this sentence.

As the drumstick moved towards the light source the shadow _____

_____

> 3.3 Transparent materials

Focus

Look at these pictures.

Which items are made from transparent materials?

Which are made from opaque materials?

1 Under each picture write 'transparent' or 'opaque'.

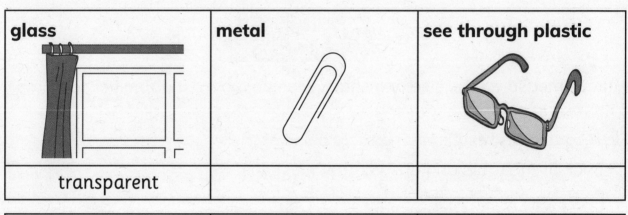

glass	metal	see through plastic
transparent		

glass lamp	egg shell	wood

rock	plastic window	magnifying glass

Practice

All sunglasses are transparent but some are more opaque than others.

2 Match the right glasses to the right environment.

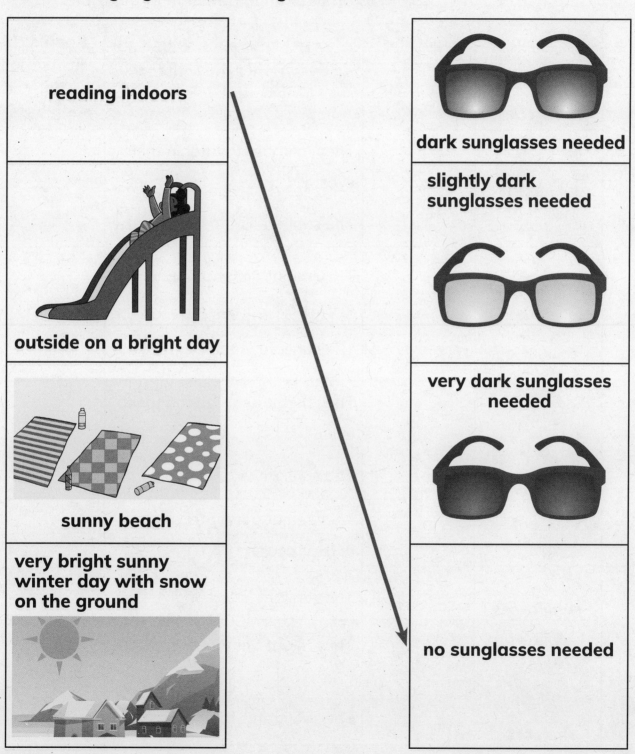

reading indoors

outside on a bright day

sunny beach

very bright sunny winter day with snow on the ground

dark sunglasses needed

slightly dark sunglasses needed

very dark sunglasses needed

no sunglasses needed

Challenge

3   What kind of eye protection do these people need?

Use a tick (✓) or cross (✗) to answer each question in the table.

Person	Does this person need eye protection?	Use a ✓ or a ✗ to say whether the sentence is true or false	Should the protection be dark like sunglasses?
visor	✓	They might get water in their eyes. ✗ The sunlight is too bright. ✓	✓
mask		They might get water in their eyes. ☐ The sunlight is too bright. ☐	
goggles		They might get water in their eyes. ☐ The sunlight is too bright. ☐	
sunglasses		They might get water in their eyes. ☐ The sunlight is too bright. ☐	
indoors		They might get water in their eyes. ☐ The sunlight is too bright. ☐	

> 3.4 Translucent materials

Focus

Here we can see sentences covered by four sheets.
Two sheets are transparent, one is translucent and one is opaque.

1   Join each word to the correct picture.

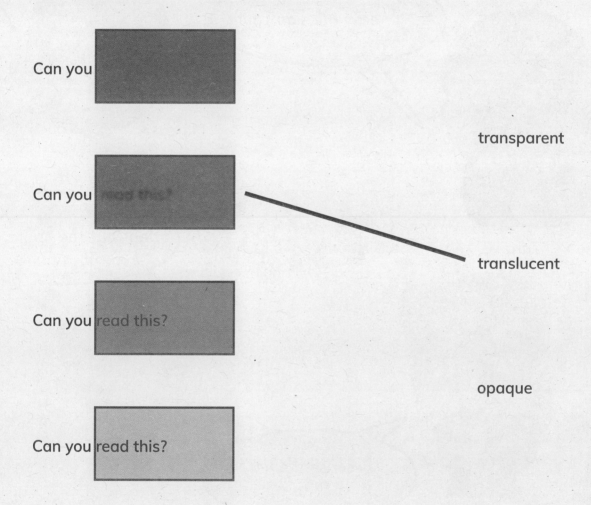

Practice

These children were asked 'Why does the Emergency sign have translucent glass with a bright lamp behind it?'

They answered like this:

... Because the glass might not break.

Marcus

... It keeps the sign cool.

Zara

EMERGENCY EXIT

... it makes the sign bright but the bright lamp is kept out of our eyes.

Arun

... Because the letters stick to it.

Sofia

2   Which child is right? Why?

Challenge

Translucent materials scatter light so that we can't see things clearly through them.

The dentist has a translucent window. It lets some light in but we cannot see clearly through the glass.

3 a Why has the dentist put translucent glass in her window?

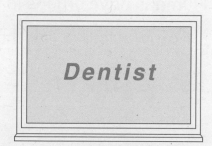

_____

_____

_____

b This light on the ceiling is covered with a translucent shade.

Why do people like to have these translucent shades on bright light bulbs?

_____

_____

c Some people put translucent glass in their front door.

Why do they do this?

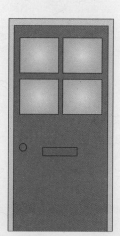

_____

_____

_____

4 Staying alive

> 4.1 Human organs

Focus

Humans have organs in their body. Each organ does a special job.

1   Draw a line to link the organ with its name.

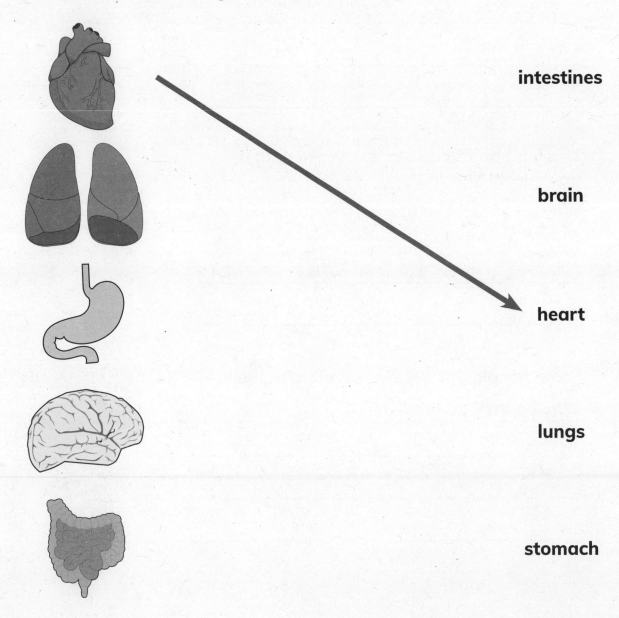

intestines

brain

heart

lungs

stomach

Practice

It is useful to know where your organs are in your body.

2   Draw these organs in the right place in the human body:
    the heart, the lungs, the brain, the stomach and intestines

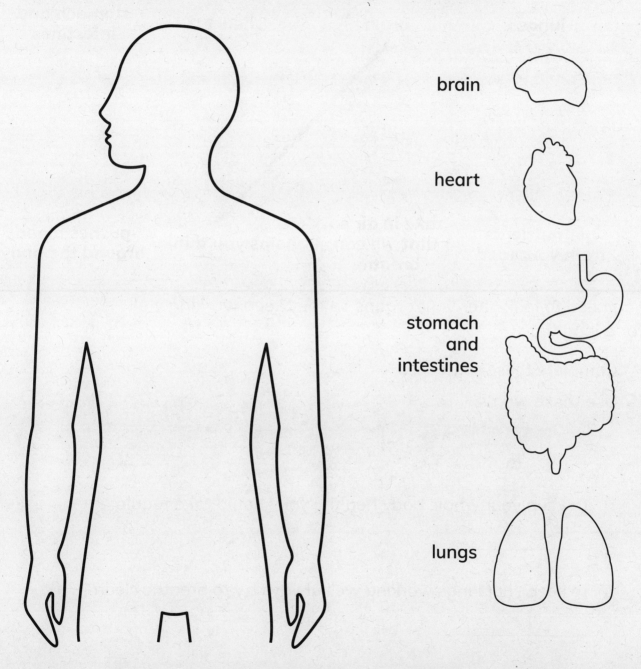

brain

heart

stomach
and
intestines

lungs

Challenge

Each of the organs in your body has an important job to do.

3 Draw an arrow to match the organ to its important job.

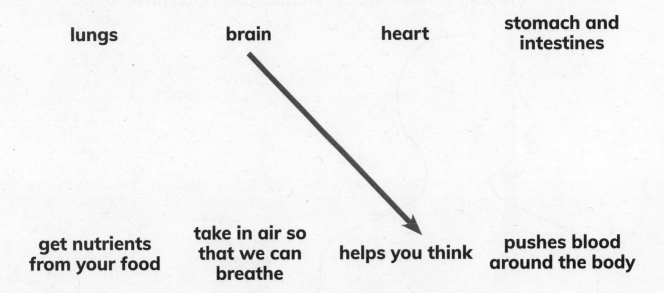

lungs   brain   heart   stomach and
                                             intestines

get nutrients   take in air so   helps you think   pushes blood
from your food   that we can   around the body
                   breathe

You need to look after your organs so they keep working well
for a long time.

4 Complete these sentences.

Use these words.

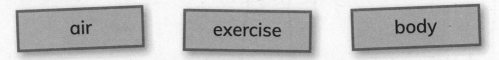

air   exercise   body

a To keep your whole body healthy you should take regular

   _____ .

b To keep your lungs working well always try to breathe clean

   _____ .

c A healthy diet will be good for all your _____ .

> 4.2 Animal groups and different life cycles

Focus

We group animals into six groups.

1 For each group draw one animal.

mammals	
reptiles	
birds	
insects	
amphibians	
fish	

Practice

All animals have a life cycle.

A life cycle diagram shows us the stages of growing.

Here is the life cycle of a horse.

The baby horse is called a foal.

The foal stays with its mother.

After two years the foal is a young horse.

After five years old we call the horse an adult.

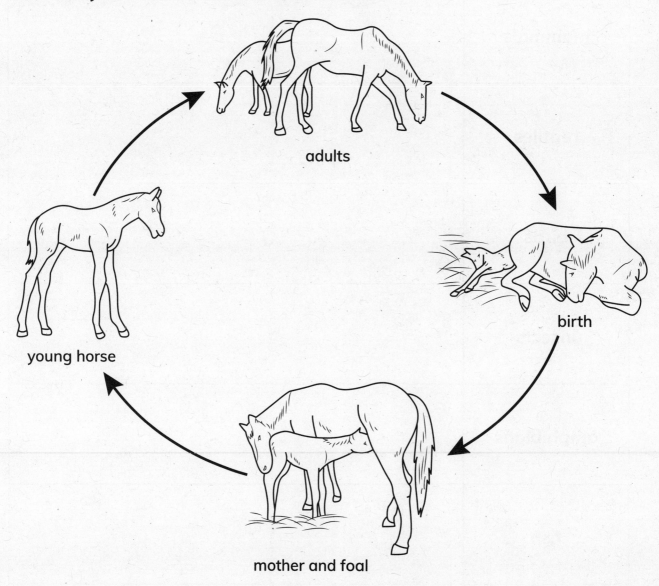

adults

birth

young horse

mother and foal

2   Look at the life cycle diagram of the horse.
    Now answer these questions.

a   What are the three stages in the life of a horse?

    _____

    _____

    _____

b   The foal is small. Is it very similar to its parents or is it very different?

    _____

c   Why does the young foal stay with its mother?

    _____

Challenge

Mammals have live young but birds, insects, amphibians and reptiles lay eggs.
This is the life cycle of a reptile, the turtle.

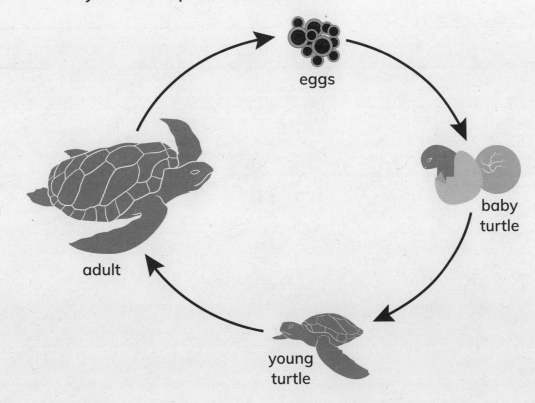

eggs

baby
turtle

young
turtle

adult

3 Put these sentences in the right order to describe this life cycle.

The young turtle grows to become an adult.

Baby turtles start to grow.

The adult lays eggs close to the sea.

Baby turtles hatch.

_____

_____

_____

4 The mother turtle lays the eggs in the beach and swims away.

Later the young turtles hatch at night and go into the sea.

Why do they hatch at night?

_____

_____

_____

> 4.3 Food chains

Focus

A food chain shows us how energy passes from one living thing to another.

Look at these living things.

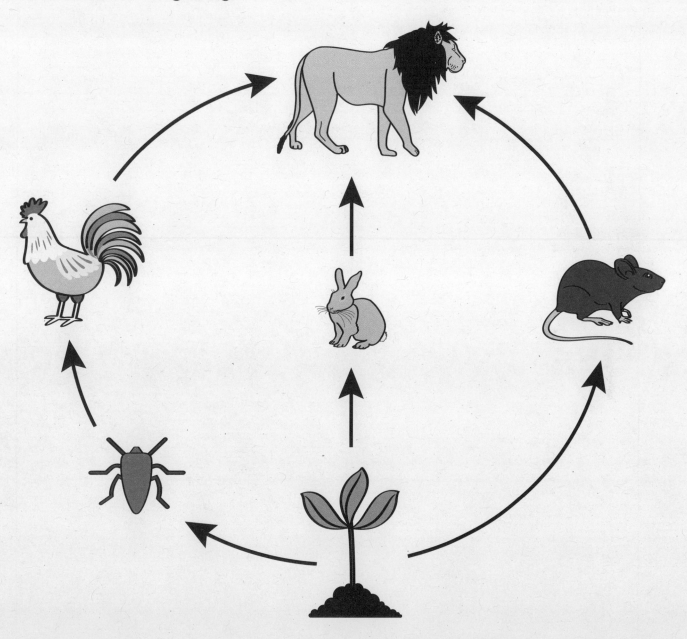

1 Draw one of the food chains in the box below.

Make sure the arrows point the right way.

Practice

The picture shows some plants and animals living in different places.

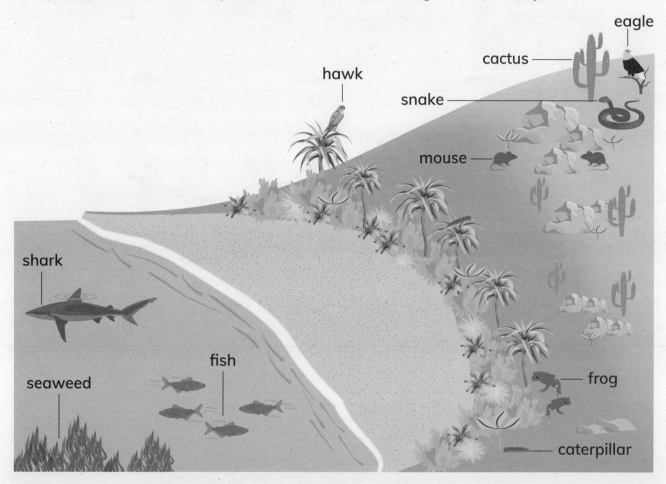

Use the words and arrows to draw a food chain for these places.

2 a A forest

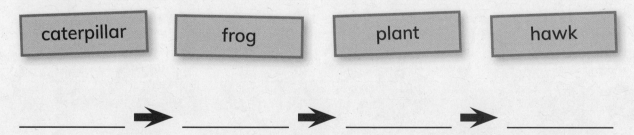

_____ ➤ _____ ➤ _____ ➤ _____

b A desert

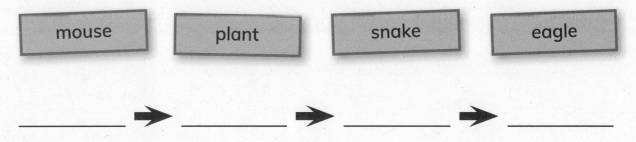

_____ → _____ → _____ → _____

c The sea

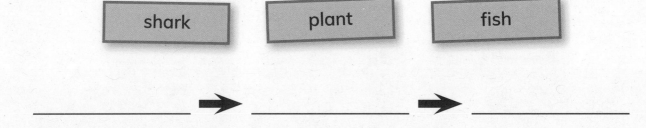

_____ → _____ → _____

3 Why does each food chain start with a plant?

_____

_____

Challenge

4 a Put each animal in a food chain with two other living things.

   b Draw and label the other living things.

_____   _____

_____   _____

_____   _____

5 Look at the six living things you added above.
Label each as a producer or consumer.

> 4.4 Fossils

Focus

Fossils show us what a living thing looked like when it was alive.

1   Complete this table.

	What kind of animal is this?	Where might it have lived?

Practice

Fossils are made when a living thing is quickly buried in mud or clay.
More mud and rock buries the living thing deeper.
Slowly the mud turns to rock.

The fish is buried for many, many years.
The soft parts disappear but the hard parts make an impression.

2 a In the left box, draw layers of rock and clay burying this dead fish.

   b In the right box, draw the fossil which might form over many years.

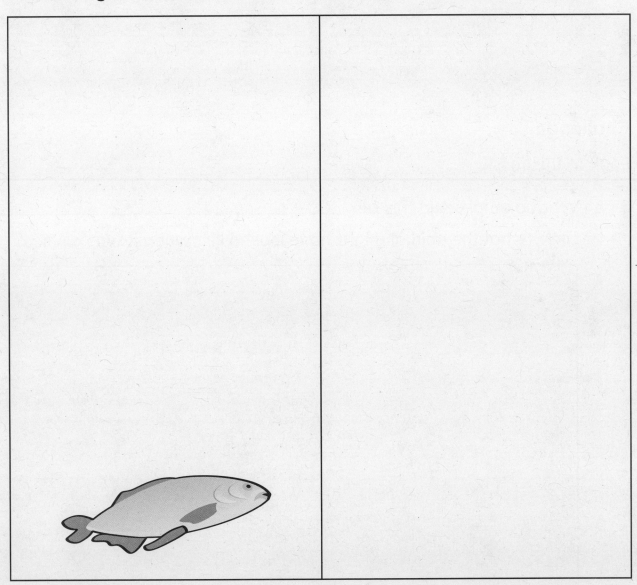

Challenge

Look at this fossil.

3 a What animal could this be? _____

   b Draw what the animal might have looked like when it was alive.

Look at these fossil teeth.

4 a What kind of animal might this be? _____

   b Why do you think that? _____

   _____

   _____

   _____

   _____

   _____

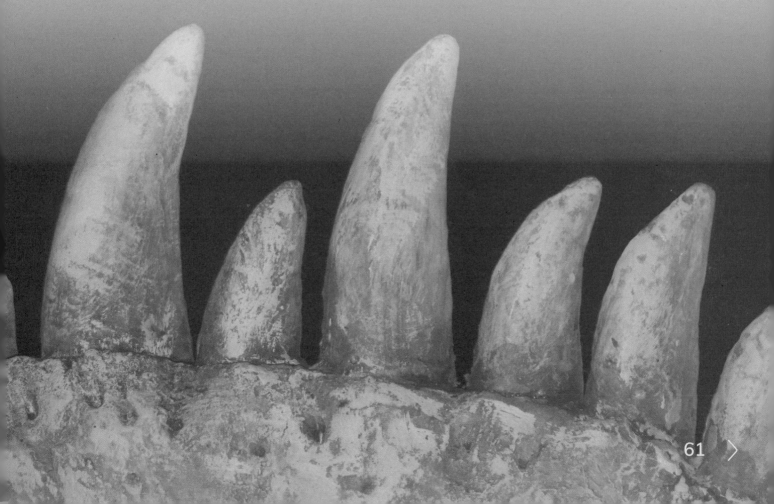

5 ▸ Forces and magnets

› 5.1 Forces and forcemeters

Focus

1 a Measure the force needed to pull each type of footwear.

   b Complete the table.

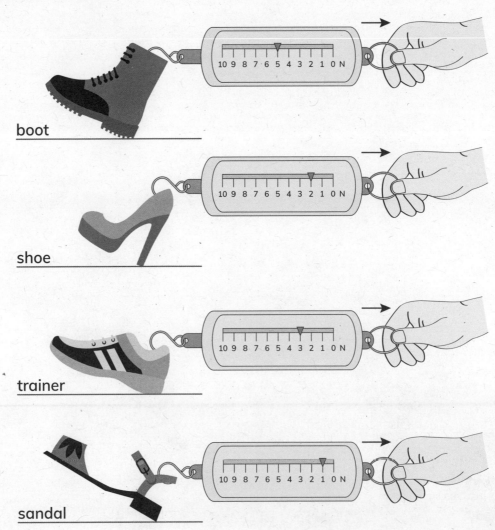

boot _____

shoe _____

trainer _____

sandal _____

Type of footwear	Force needed to pull it

Practice

2 Look at the pictures in the Focus exercise.

a Which type of footwear needed the biggest force to pull it?

_____

b Which type of footwear needed the smallest force to pull it?

_____

c How much more force was needed to pull the trainer than the sandal?

_____

d Is Marcus correct?

The shoe is easier to pull than the boot.

_____

_____

Challenge

3 Draw lines to match these objects to their weight.

school bag

1N

3 bananas

5N

apple

10N

table

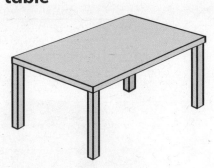

20N

chair

50N

> 5.2 Gravity

Focus

1 Draw arrows to show which way these footballs would fall.

One has been done for you.

Practice

2   Which of these needs gravity?

Tick (✓) the correct answer.

□ Uses gravity

□ Does not use gravity

□ Uses gravity

□ Does not use gravity

□ Uses gravity

□ Does not use gravity

□ Uses gravity

□ Does not use gravity

□ Uses gravity

□ Does not use gravity

□ Uses gravity

□ Does not use gravity

Challenge

3 Tick (✓) to show whether these sentences are true or false.

a Gravity pulls things towards the centre of the Earth. True ☐ False ☐

b Down is the same direction everywhere on Earth. True ☐ False ☐

c Weight is measured in grams or kilograms. True ☐ False ☐

d Gravity makes objects have weight. True ☐ False ☐

e Gravity pushes aeroplanes upwards. True ☐ False ☐

> 5.3 Friction

Focus

1 Label these forces.

   a Use these words.

   | push |

   | friction |

   b Use these words.

   | friction |

   | pull |

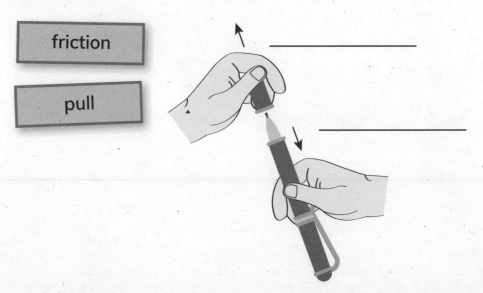

c Use these words.

friction

gravity

Practice

2 Draw and label an arrow on each picture to show the direction of the friction.

a Pulling a trolley.

b Sliding on a smooth floor.

c Pulling on a rope.

3 What does friction do to moving objects?

_____

_____

_____

Challenge

William investigates the question 'Which surface has the most friction?'

He measures friction on different surfaces to find the answer.

Here are his results.

Surface	Friction (N)
Wood	10
Carpet	20
Sand	18

This is his conclusion.

The friction on the carpet was 20 N.

4 a Why is this not a good conclusion?

_____

   b Write a better conclusion.

_____

_____

› 5.4 Amazing magnets

Focus

1   Label these diagrams and colour the poles of the magnets.

Use the words attract and repel. Use a N for a north pole and a S for a south pole.

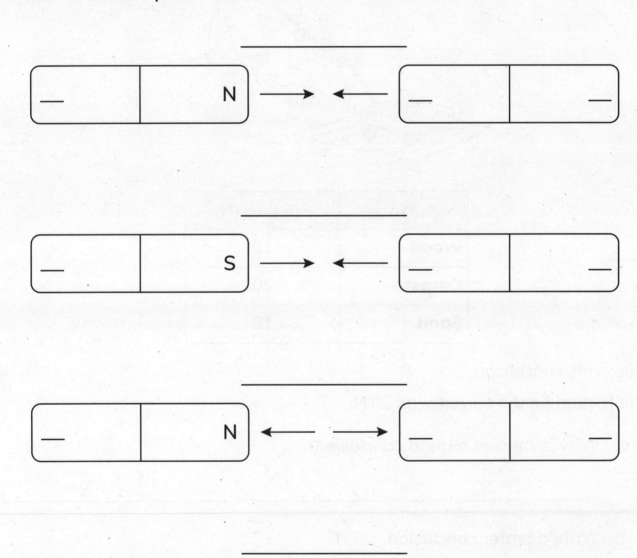

Practice

2 Sofia writes what she found out about magnets.

Not all of her sentences are correct. Mark the sentences with a tick (✓) or a cross (✗) to show whether they are correct.

1. A magnet has a north pole and a south pole. ☐

2. Two north poles attract each other. ☐

3. Only south poles attract metal paper clips. ☐

4. A north pole and a south pole attract each other. ☐

5. Magnets repel non-magnetic materials. ☐

Challenge

If you know the poles of one magnet you can work out the poles of another.

3 How would you use this bar magnet to work out which pole is north, and which is south on the horseshoe magnet?

Use these words in your answer.

repel   attract

_____

_____

_____

_____

_____

_____

› 5.5 Magnetic materials

Focus

1 a Draw a line from the magnet to the magnetic objects.

   b Put a cross (✗) next to the non-magnetic objects.

Practice

2 Classify these materials by writing them in the correct place in the table.

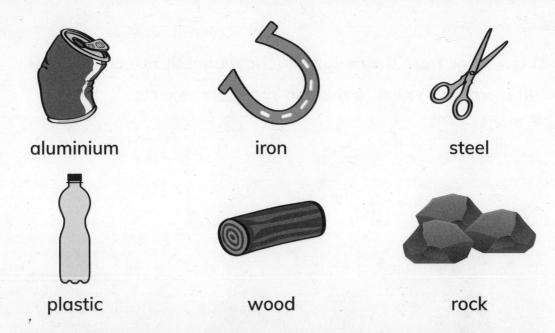

aluminium   iron   steel

plastic   wood   rock

Magnetic	Non-magnetic

3 Choose the right words to finish these sentences.

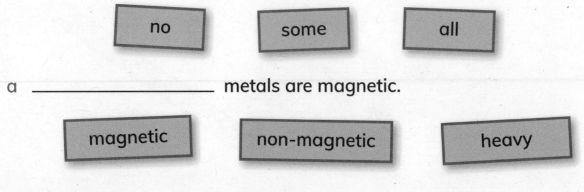

| no | some | all |

a _____ metals are magnetic.

| magnetic | non-magnetic | heavy |

b Materials that are not metal are _____ .

Challenge

4   Use science words about magnets to solve this crossword.

1   One end of a magnet. (4 letters)

2   A word for materials that are not attracted to a magnet. (11 letters)

3   A metal that is non-magnetic. (9 letters)

4   An object that attracts some metals. (6 letters)

5   A word for materials that are attracted to a magnet. (8 letters)

6   A metal that is magnetic. (5 letters)

7   Pull towards a magnet. (7 letters)

8   Push away from a magnet. (5 letters)

6 The Earth and the Moon

> 6.1 The shape of the Earth, Sun and Moon

Focus

1 Group these objects by shape by writing their names in the correct part of the table.

Earth

can

Moon

cardboard box

book

pencil

football

Sun

Sphere	Cuboid	Cylinder

Practice

2 Look at this fact file about the Earth, Sun and Moon and answer the questions.

Name	Shape	Material	Size (km)	Mass (kg)	Gravity (N/kg)
Sun	sphere	gas	1 392 684	1 989 100 000 000 billion billion	293
Earth	sphere	rock and water	12 756	5 972 190 billion billion	10
Moon	sphere	rock	3 475	641 693 billion billion	2

a What shape is the Moon? _____

b What material is the Sun made of? _____

c Which has the biggest mass? _____

d Which has the strongest gravity? _____

e How many times stronger is gravity on Earth than on the Moon?

   _____

Challenge

3 Read this information and answer the questions.

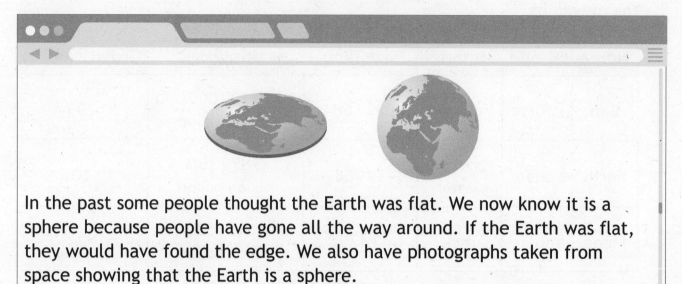

In the past some people thought the Earth was flat. We now know it is a sphere because people have gone all the way around. If the Earth was flat, they would have found the edge. We also have photographs taken from space showing that the Earth is a sphere.

a Write two things that show us that the Earth is not flat.

_____

_____

_____

_____

b Why are the Earth, the Moon and the Sun all spheres?

_____

_____

c Why might people think that the Earth was flat?

_____

_____

> 6.2 The Moon

Focus

1 Are these sentences true or false?

  a The Earth and the Moon are both spheres. _____

  b The Moon is larger than the Earth. _____

  c The Moon goes around the Earth. _____

  d The Moon's orbit is a circle. _____

  e The Moon takes one day to orbit the Earth. _____

Practice

Arun and Zara are modelling
the Earth and the Moon.
Zara is holding a football
and Arun is holding
an orange.

2 a What is the Moon in this model? _____

  b What is the Earth in this model? _____

  c Who should move in this model? _____

  d Write one way the model is similar to the real Earth and Moon.

  _____

  e Write one way the model is different to the real Earth and Moon.

  _____

Challenge

Marcus is making a scale model of the planets in our Solar System.

He is using the scale 1000 km = 1 cm

How big should each planet be in the model?

3 a Fill in the table to show how big each planet should be in the model.

Two of them have been done for you.

Planet	Size of real planet (km)	Size of model planet (cm)
Mercury	5000	
Venus	12 000	
Earth	13 000	13
Mars	7000	
Jupiter	140 000	
Saturn	116 000	
Uranus	51 000	
Neptune	49 000	49

b Which is the biggest planet? _____

c Which is the smallest planet? _____

d The Sun is 1 390 000 km across. How big would the Sun be in this model?

_____

❯ 6.3 The phases of the Moon

Focus

1 Write the full names of these phases of the Moon.

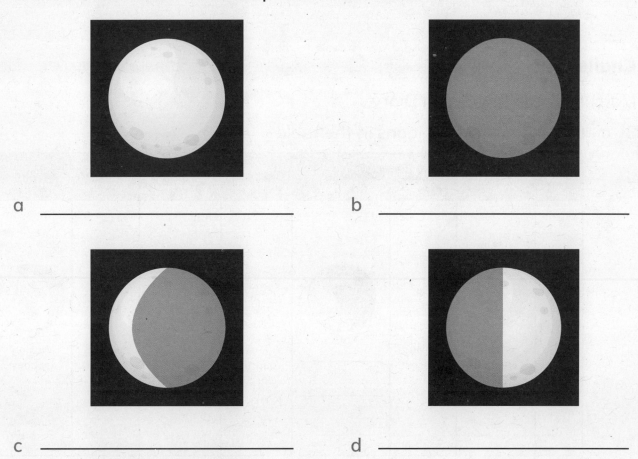

a _____

b _____

c _____

d _____

e _____

Practice

2 Draw each of these phases of the Moon.

  a   crescent Moon   b   full Moon   c   gibbous Moon

Challenge

Marcus is making a Moon Diary.

3 a Draw the missing Moons in the table

Date	Monday 3rd April	Tuesday 4th April	Wednesday 5th April	Thursday 6th April	Friday 7th April	Saturday 8th April	Sunday 9th April
Observation	Waxing crescent	Waxing crescent	_____	First quarter	_____	Waxing gibbous	Waxing gibbous
Rises:	1.36am	2.51am	4.00am	5.00am	5.50am	6.29am	7.01am
Sets:	10.48pm	11.21pm	12.00pm	12.53pm	1.52pm	2.56pm	4.03pm

  b   Write the missing names in the table.

  c   How long was the Moon in the sky on Wednesday? _____

  d   Does the Moon set earlier or later every day? _____

  e   How much later did the Moon rise on Friday than on Thursday?

  _____